Heart Hiders Color

Parent/Teacher Guide

Welcome to the wonderful world of Scripture memorization! The *Heart Hiders Coloring Book* is a great way to teach young children to hide God's Word in their hearts. This reproducible coloring book contains 58 foundational verses essential to building our Christian faith.

Please feel free to make as many copies as you like for either classroom or home use. When copying this book, set your copier at 150% and choose the 11"x17" paper selection. You will then have poster size Bible verses that kids learn as they color. Teachers, you can make your own posters for the class to memorize. Just make some 11"x17" copies, color them or have your class color them and then laminate them. You will have bright, colorful posters to display all year long.

Don't forget! This coloring book is just one of an entire line of Heart Hiders products, including *Heart Hiders Book Volume 1*, *Heart Hiders Flash Cards and Heart Hiders Bookmarks*.

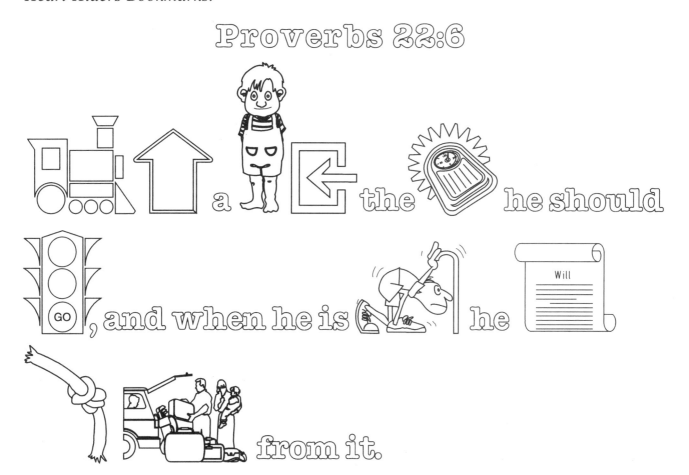

Train up a **child in** the **way** he should **go**, and when he is **old** he **will not depart** from it. NKJV

Heart Hiders Coloring Book
Copyright © 1998 by Anthony S. Thiessen
All rights reserved.

Scripture taken from the New American Standard Bible ®,
Copyright © the Lockman Foundation 1960, 1962, 1963, 1968, 1971, 1972,
1973, 1975, 1977, 1995 Used by permission

Scripture taken from The Holy Bible, New International Version (North American
Edition), Copyright © 1973, 1978, 1984 by the International Bible Society. Used by
permission of Zondervan Publishing House.

Scripture quotation marked NKJV are taken from the New Kings James Bible, copyright © 1979 1980 1982 Thomas Nelson Inc. Used by permission. All rights
reserved.

ISBN 0-9660489-1-1
Printed in the United States of America

Off The Curb Publishing
306-N West El Norte Parkway Ste. 352
Escondido, Ca. 92026
(800)-294-2397   www.hearthiders.com

Psalm 119:11

**I have hidden your word in my heart that
I might not sin against you.** NIV

Psalm 119:105

Your [book] is a [lamp] [2]
my [feet] and a [bulb] [2]
my [path].

Your **word** is a **lamp to** my **feet** and a
light to my **path**. NKJV

John 15:5

"I am the **vine, you are** the **branches.** He **who** abides **in Me,** and **I in** him, **bears** much **fruit; for without** Me **you can** do **nothing."** NKJV

John 3:16

For God so loved the world that He gave His one and only Son, that whoever believes in Him shall not perish but have eternal life. NIV

Heart Hiders www.hearthiders.com (800)294-2397

1 John 1:9

If we [ ]fess [R] [◎]s, He is [dog/shoe] and [justice] [2] [4] [hand] us [R] [◎]s and [2] [SOAP] us from all

un [ ]ness.

If we confess our sins, He is **faithful** and **just to forgive** us **our sins** and **to cleanse** us from all **unrighteousness.** NKJV

Heart Hiders www.hearthiders.com (800)294-2397

Romans 1:16

For I am not ashamed of the **gospel** of Christ, **for** it is the **power** of **God to** salvation **for everyone who believes.** NKJV

Galatians 5:22,23a

But the 🍇 of the 🔥 is ❤ LoVe,

joy, ☮, [patience], kindness

[goodness]ness, [faithful]ness,

[gentle]ness, self-[con]trol.

But the fruit of the Spirit is love, joy, peace, patience, kindness, goodness, faithfulness, gentleness, self-control. NASB

Heart Hiders www.hearthiders.com (800)294-2397

Psalm 23:1

The LORD is my 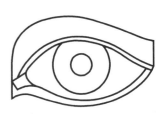,

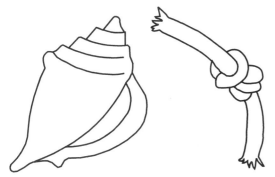   want.

The LORD is my shepherd, I shall not be in want. NIV

---

1 John 4:19

   cause He

We LoVe Him cause He

 d us.

We love Him because He first loved us. NKJV

Heart Hiders www.hearthiders.com (800)294-2397

Romans 8:31

What then **shall** we **say to** these **things**? If **God** is **for** us, **who can be against** us? NKJV

John 14:6

Jesus said **to** him, "**I am** the **way**, and the **truth**, and the **life**; **no one** comes to the **Father**, but **through** Me."
NASB

Heart Hiders www.hearthiders.com (800)294-2397

Romans 5:8

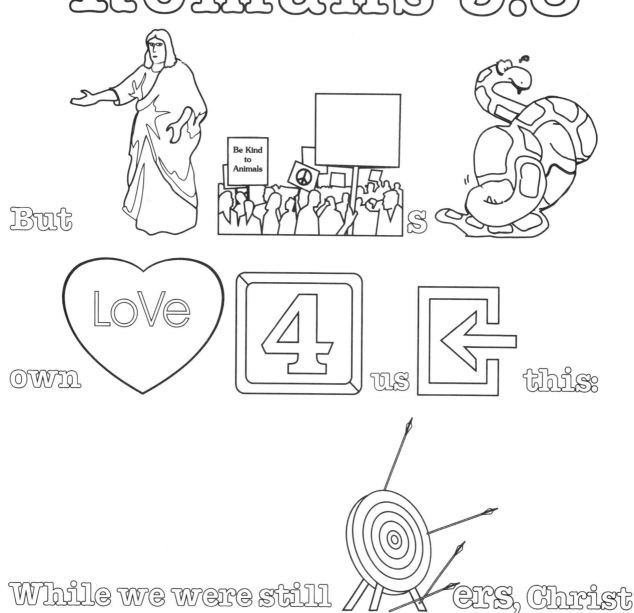

But 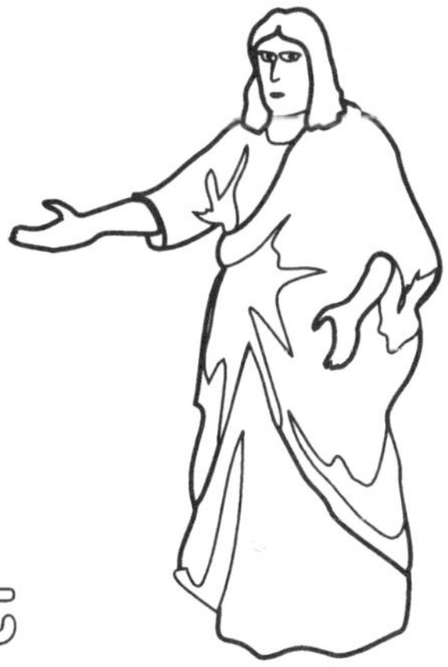 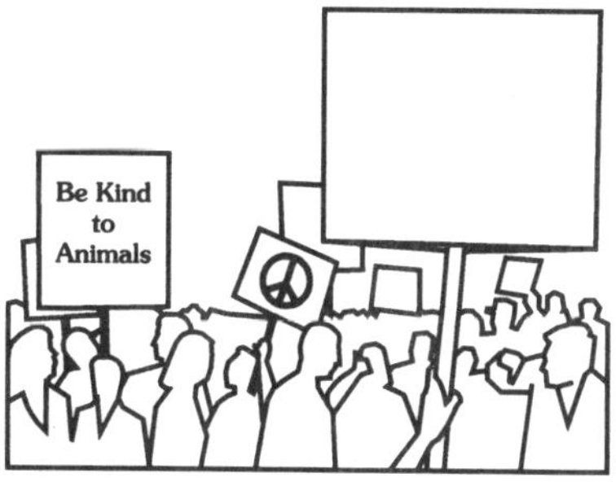

s 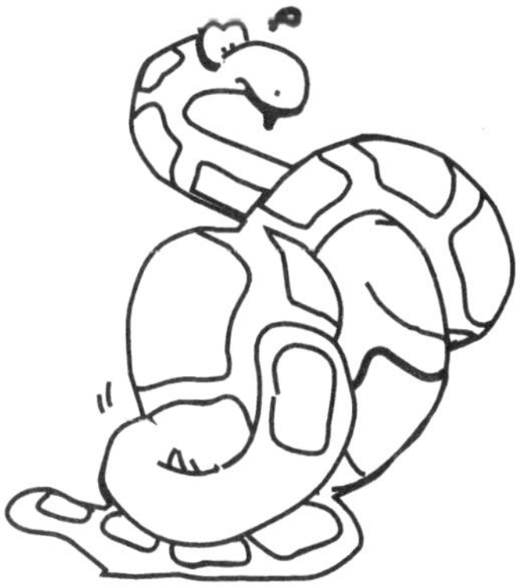

own 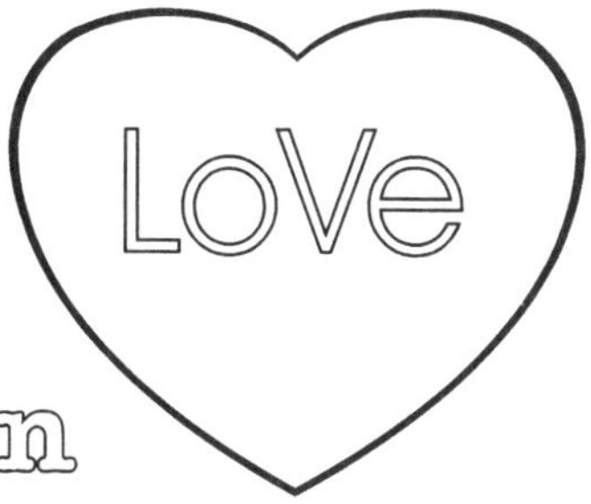

us 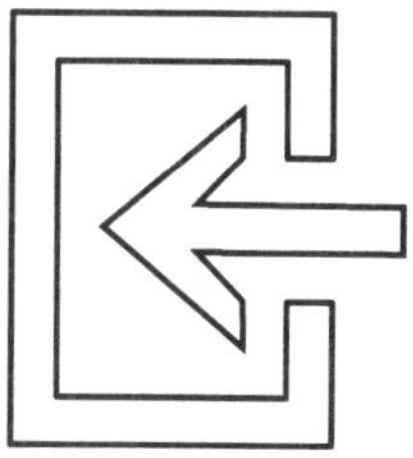 this:

While we were still 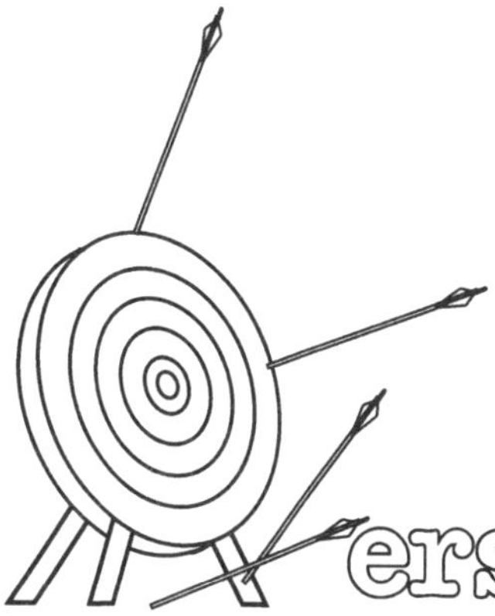 ers, Christ

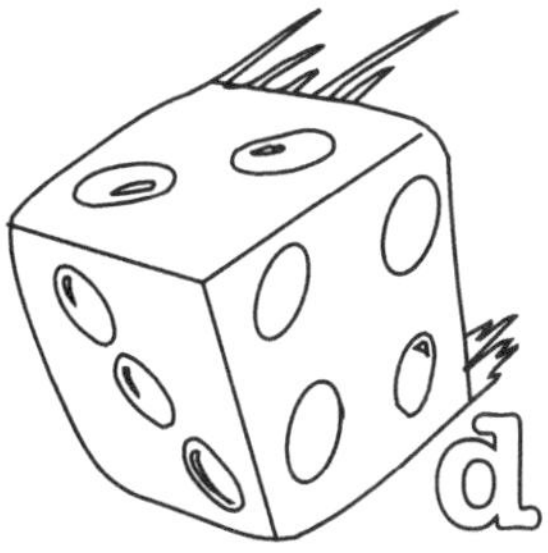 d 

us.

But **God demonstrates His** own **love for** us **in** this:
While we were still **sinners**, Christ **died for** us. NIV

Heart Hiders www.hearthiders.com (800)294-2397

Colossians 3:20

 , 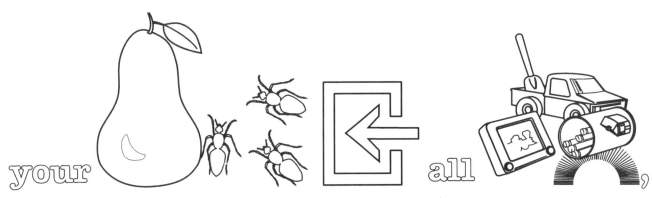 o d 2

your 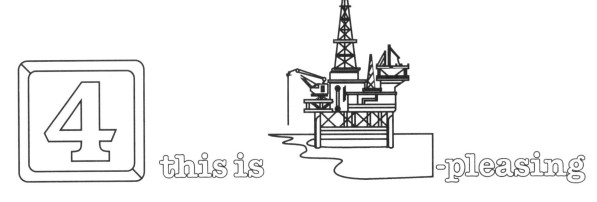 all ,

4 this is -pleasing

2 the LORD.

Children, be obedient to your parents in all things, for this is well-pleasing to the LORD. NASB

Heart Hiders www.hearthiders.com (800)294-2397

Proverbs 3:12

For whom the LORD **loves** He **corrects, just** as a **father** the **son in whom** he **delights**. NKJV

Heart Hiders www.hearthiders.com (800)294-2397

Psalm 100:2

the LORD with gladness;

come 4

with

Serve the LORD with **gladness**; come **before His presence** with **singing**. NKJV

Heart Hiders www.hearthiders.com (800)294-2397

Mark 16:15

And He said **to** them, "**Go into** all the **world** and **preach** the **gospel to** every creature." NKJV

Heart Hiders www.hearthiders.com (800)294-2397

Psalm 118:24

This is the *Day* the LORD has

; we ☐ **Rejoice!** and

gl ☐ it.

This is the **day** the LORD has **made**; we **will rejoice** and **be glad in** it. NKJV

Heart Hiders www.hearthiders.com (800)294-2397

Romans 3:23

For all have **sinned** and **fall** short of the **glory** of **God**. NASB

Philippians 4:13

I **can** do everything **through** Him **who gives** me **strength**. NIV

1 Peter 5:7

all your anxiety   Him

cause He **CARE**s

4 U.

Cast all your anxiety **on** Him **because**
He **cares for you**. NIV

Heart Hiders www.hearthiders.com (800)294-2397

Proverbs 7:1

My ___, keep My ___ S, and ___ my ___ s with ___

U.

My son, keep My **words**, and **treasure** My **commands within you**. NKJV

Heart Hiders www.hearthiders.com (800)294-2397

Romans 6:23

For the wages of **sin** is **death**, but the **gift** of **God** is **eternal life** in Christ **Jesus our** LORD. NKJV

Colossians 3:23

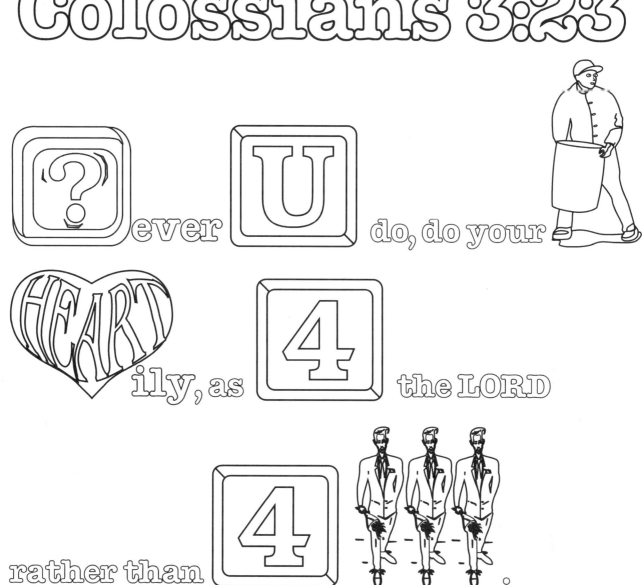

[?]ever [U] do, do your ❤️HEART ily, as [4] the LORD rather than [4] .

Whatever you do, do your **work heartily,** as **for** the LORD rather than **for men.** NASB

Heart Hiders www.hearthiders.com (800)294-2397

Proverbs 15:1

A gentle answer turns away wrath, but a harsh
word stirs up anger. NASB

Revelation 3:20

"Be hold 👁 I at the 🚪 and . If any 1️⃣ s My voice and OPEN s the 🚪, 👁 Will COMe ⬅️2️⃣ him and with him,

and he with Me."

"Behold I stand at the **door** and **knock. If anyone hears** My voice and **opens** the **door, I will come in to** him and **dine** with him, and he with Me." NKJV

Romans 8:28

And we know that [←] all  s 4 the of

those LoVe Him, have

2

And we know that **in all things God works for** the **good** of those **who love** Him, **who** have **been called according to His purpose**. NIV

Heart Hiders www.hearthiders.com (800)294-2397

Matthew 7:12

So in everything, do **to** others **what you would** have them do **to you, for** this **sums up** the **Law** and the prophets. NIV

Heart Hiders www.hearthiders.com (800)294-2397

Matthew 22:37,38

And He said  him, "

 the LORD your  with all

your  and with all your , and

with all your  ." This is the gr

and  most   ment.

And He said to him, "You shall love the LORD your God with all your heart and with all your soul, and with all your mind." "This is the great and foremost commandment." NASB

Heart Hiders www.hearthiders.com (800)294-2397

Psalm 23:4

Yea, though **I walk through** the **valley** of the **shadow** of **death, I will fear no evil; for You are** with me; Your **rod** and Your **staff** they **comfort** me. NKJV

Heart Hiders www.hearthiders.com (800)294-2397

1 John 5:14

this is the [bars] fidence that we have [arrow] Him, that if we anything [accordion] [2]

[turtle/snake], He Will, He [man] S us.

Now this is the **confidence** that we have **in** Him, that if we **ask** anything **according to His will**, He **hears** us.

NKJV

John 1:12

But as many as ⟨mailbox⟩ Him, ② them

He ⟨offering box⟩ the right ② ⟨bee⟩ come

⟨children⟩ of ⟨Jesus⟩ , ⟨scales⟩ ② those

⟨owl⟩ ⟨bee⟩ ⟨leaf⟩ ⟨arrow⟩ His ANDY.

But as many as **received** Him, **to** them He **gave** the right **to become children** of **God, even to** those **who believe in His name**. NASB

Heart Hiders www.hearthiders.com (800)294-2397

John 10:10b

" (eye) have COMe that they

May have (heart) , and that they

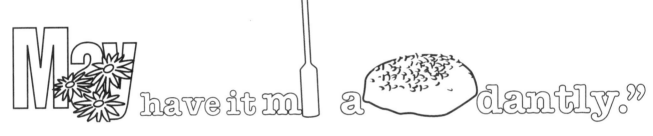

May have it m(bat) a (loaf)dantly."

"I have **come** that they **may** have **life**, and that they **may** have it **more abundantly."** NKJV

Heart Hiders www.hearthiders.com (800)294-2397

Proverbs 3:5,6

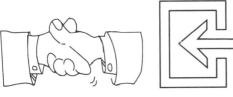 the LORD with all your

 , and 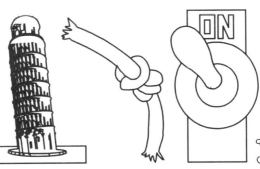 your own

ing;  all your s

 Him, and He

your s.

Trust in the LORD with all your **heart,** and **lean not on** your own **understanding; in** all your **ways acknowledge** Him, and He **shall direct** your **paths.**
NKJV

1 Corinthians 16:14

Let all that [U] do [LoVe] done with ♥.

Let all that you do be done with love. NKJV

Psalm 56:3

When 👁 [M] afraid, 👁

When [Will] 🤝 ← [U] .

When I am afraid, I will trust in You. NIV

Psalm 9:10

And those 🦉 know Your ANDY

Will 🏃 their 🤝 ⬅️

U; 4 U, LORD, have

4 saken those 🦉 🕵️

U.

And those who know your name will put their trust in you; for you, LORD, have not forsaken those who seek You. NKJV

Heart Hiders www.hearthiders.com (800)294-2397

Hebrews 13:8

Christ is the same

yesterDay, 2 Day, and 4 ever.

Jesus Christ is the same **yesterday**, **today** and **forever**.
NKJV

2 Corinthians 5:17

There [4], if any [1] is [←]

Christ, he is a NEW creation;

have a ;

hold, all have

come NEW .

Therefore, if **anyone** is **in** Christ, he is a **new** creation; **old things** have **passed away**; **behold**, all **things** have **become new**. NKJV

Heart Hiders www.hearthiders.com (800)294-2397

Ephesians 4:32

And **be** kind **to one** another, **tenderhearted**, **forgiving** each other, **just** as **God in** Christ also has **forgiven you**. NASB

Heart Hiders www.hearthiders.com (800)294-2397

1 John 3:17,18

If any [1] has material possessions

and [C]s [turtle] brother [←] need

but has [⊘] pity [switch ON] him, how [can]

the ♥LoVe♥ of [Jesus] [bee] [←] him? [deer]

[kids], let us [arm] ♥LoVe♥ with [Bible]s

[mouth] but with actions and [←] [pilgrim].

If **anyone** has material possessions and **sees his** brother **in** need but has **no** pity **on** him, how **can** the **love** of **God be in** him? **Dear children,** let us **not love** with **words or tongue** but with actions and **in truth.** NIV

Jeremiah 32:27

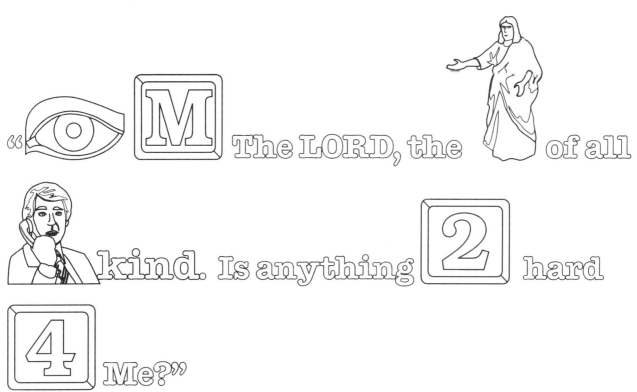

"I am the LORD, the **God** of all **mankind**. Is anything **too** hard **for** Me?" NIV

Psalm 118:6

The LORD is with me; **I will not be** afraid. **What can man** do **to** me? NIV

Heart Hiders www.hearthiders.com (800)294-2397

Colossians 3:13

Bear with each other and **forgive whatever** grievances **you may** have **against one** another. **Forgive** as the LORD **forgave you**. NIV

Heart Hiders www.hearthiders.com (800)294-2397

Isaiah 41:10

So do **not fear, for I am** with **you**; do **not be dismayed, for I am** your **God.** **I will strengthen you** and help **you**; **I will uphold you** with my **righteous** right **hand.** NIV

Heart Hiders www.hearthiders.com (800)294-2397

Ephesians 2:8,9

For by **grace you** have **been saved** through faith; and that **not** of yourselves, it is the **gift** of **God**; **not** as a result of **works**, that **no one** should boast. NASB

Heart Hiders www.hearthiders.com (800)294-2397

Psalm 37:4,5

De[light] yourself [in] the LORD; and He [will] [give] [you] the desires of your [heart]. Co[mmit] your [way] [2] the LORD, [trust] also [in] Him, and He [will] do it.

Delight yourself **in** the LORD; and He **will give you** the desires of your **heart**. **Commit** your **way to** the LORD, **trust also in** Him, and He **will** do it. NASB

Heart Hiders www.hearthiders.com (800)294-2397

Proverbs 13:1

A  heeds

's , but a scoffer does

  rebuke.

A **wise son** heeds **his father's instruction**, but a scoffer does **not listen to** rebuke. NKJV

Psalm 121:7,8

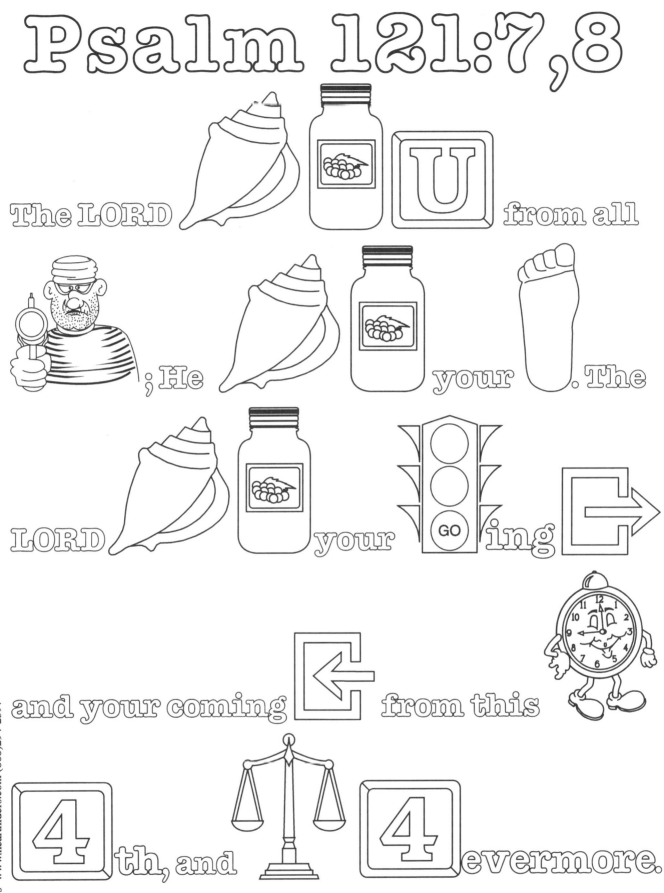

The LORD **shall preserve you** from all **evil**; He **shall preserve** your **soul**. The Lord **shall preserve** your **going out** and your coming **in** from this **time forth**. and **even forevermore**. NKJV

Proverbs 3:1,2

My ☀, do 4 get my

Law , but let your HEART keep my

s; 4 length of Days

and  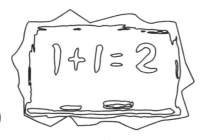 and  they

Will 1+1=2 2 U.

My son, do not forget my law, but let your heart keep my commands; for length of days and long life and peace they will add to you. NKJV

Heart Hiders www.hearthiders.com (800)294-2397

Proverbs 3:3,4

Let [knot] mercy and [tree-forsake] 4 sake

U ; [bind] them around your [giraffe-neck],

[write] them [switch-ON] the [tablet] of your

[HEART], and [sew-so] find [favor] and high

[tea-e] [enter-in] the sight of [God] and [man].

Let **not** mercy and **truth forsake you**; **bind** them around your **neck**, **write** them **on** the **tablet** of your **heart**, and **so** find **favor** and high **esteem in** the sight of **God** and **man**. NKJV

Heart Hiders   www.hearthiders.com (800)294-2397